CONVERSION

CONVERSION

by

Erik Routley

FORTRESS PRESS • PHILADELPHIA

Second printing 1962
First paperback edition 1978

Copyright © 1960 by Fortress Press

Library of Congress Cataloging in Publication Data

Routley, Erik.
  Conversion.

  1. Conversion. I. Title.
BT780.R66 1977   248′.24   77-20298
ISBN 0-8006-1327-9

6505J77   Printed in the United States of America   1-1327

CONTENTS

WHAT IS CONVERSION?

In the Bible, "convert" means "turn." It is fairly often used in the religious sense, but you see its dramatic force if you look at the one place in the King James Version where it is used without that sense. In Isa. 60:5 it is written, "The abundance of the sea shall be converted unto thee"; there the picture is of a great fleet of merchant ships bound for some foreign port being, at the word of command, turned off its course and brought into a home port, captured, with all its wealth and splendor, and now moving, not *there*, but *here*.

In this word "turn" there is always a dramatic force. It is always, whether the original is Hebrew or Greek, a decisive turning—stopping in your tracks, attending to an order, and then turning and making for the new destination. And in the Christian teaching about conversion, all those things are implied. When Peter in his sermon to the Jews recorded in Acts 3 said (v. 19), "Repent therefore, and turn again," he meant something quite decisive, such as, "Stop! You are moving in the wrong direction. Attend to the facts which I am giving you. Then turn and take your new journey."

When we talk about conversion this, and no more, is what we are talking about. We are not talking about the journey itself; we are talking about the act of turning from the old route to the new one. But, of course, if we are to say anything about even that, we must have some idea about the destination toward which the new route leads. If we have that, then we shall in the end be able to judge more clearly what was wrong with the old route. Having made that judgment, we shall perhaps be able to help others by showing them the defects of the old route and the destination of the new one. These are the subjects with which this book is designed to deal.

A PARABLE

Suppose there was a man born in Chicago who says to himself at the age of, say, eighteen, "I will go and seek my fortune. I will leave this city." He knows he must go, and go alone. Where in the whole American continent shall he go, and why? Perhaps he will just start walking along Route 41 and see where that takes him. That would be a romantic thing to do, but the chances are that before he has been walking for a week he will run into bad weather or his boots will begin to pinch, and he will say, "There is no future in this," and look for a lift back to Chicago. There was nothing ahead of him to draw him on. But suppose somebody has told him that there is big money in Pittsburgh. Then, for self-interest's sake, he will probably press on, never mind the weather or the discomfort. It is not unlikely that along the way he will meet people who say, "Pittsburgh? No, no. Philadelphia is the place you want." "Philadelphia? Boy, have you never heard of Los Angeles?" "Los Angeles? You'll never make anything of that. New York's the place." He may go zigzagging all over the country from coast to coast in pursuit of self-interest. He may even end up in Chicago again.

But now suppose that on his way out of Chicago he meets somebody who says, "Your father is in Nashville, and he is asking for you." What might happen then? I can think of several turns the conversation might take: (1) "My father? I've never seen him. He doesn't want me." (2) "My father? He deserted my mother when I was a kid; and she died, and I've nowhere to go, but I don't want to meet him again." (3) "My father? Do you mean to say that he wants me, and I've been wrong all these years about him? Why, I thought he'd forgotten me!" (4) "My father? I've been wanting him all these years, but I've never known where he was. Put me on the road to Nashville this minute."

Whether he was just walking aimlessly, or whether he was making for Pittsburgh, the stranger's news will stop him in his tracks. And whether the news brings out a reaction of contempt, grievance, surprise, or delight, if the stranger can satisfy him (a) that his father does really live in Nashville, (b) that his father wants him, and (c) that all his ideas of his father forgetting him and despising him and ill-treating his mother are quite wrong, sooner or later that young man will get to his destination.

Actually, the stranger will not be able to *prove* any of those things; you cannot prove that kind of thing—at any rate you cannot prove b and c. You can only persuade. The stranger can only infect the traveler with his own belief and assurance. But if he has done that, and if you can see the traveler taking his first steps down the new road, leaving the old road behind, you can call that traveler a converted man.

Now that is a parable. It is no more. "Chicago" is

the child's dependent existence, in which major decisions are always taken by somebody else. The urge to travel is the urge to leave behind that childish state, which is natural to every man. Pittsburgh and Philadelphia and Los Angeles and New York symbolize—well, they symbolize just what you care to attach to them. Plenty of important things are left out by this parable, but the picture of conversion, and the picture of contempt, grievance, surprise, or joy which are reactions to good news are authentic; so is the personal nature of the good news; and so is the picture of the conversion.

The bad weather and the tight shoes will be no less noticeable on the new road than they were on the old one. The traveler is going to have trouble. He is going to wish he had never listened to the stranger. He is going to look for a signpost back to Pittsburgh, or maybe to Chicago. The stranger may go a little way with him, but he can't go the whole way because his business may be elsewhere. There will be others who help him along the way. In between times he may have doubts even about the authenticity of the good news, and about his wisdom in accepting it. He may run off the road and find himself in North Carolina being told by somebody, "Brother, you'll have to go back and turn right where you turned left, and that'll put you right for Nashville."

The whole process of keeping, or being kept, to the road, is sanctification. As the traveler gets nearer, though he hardly knows it, he is being made more fit to arrive. Had he been confronted by his father twenty miles outside Chicago, he might have turned about and gone irretrievably back to his apartment, he might have dithered and doubted, he might have run screaming from what he thought was a ghost. (This principle is, I believe, implied in much of Old Testament experience, especially in the passage Exod. 33:17-23.) But by the time he gets there, what with the chance of sorting it all out in his own mind and the discipline of having to pass through the hazards of the journey, he may well be ready to be a good citizen and, what is much more important to him, to face the searing experience of his father's forgiveness.

One of the things that will happen will be that he will see more clearly as he goes along what the shape of his journey has been. He will see his emergence from Chicago, *plus* his redirection onto the right road, as a rescue —rescue from a kind of bondage, and from the futility of a self-interested life. The technical word for that rescue is "salvation." And he will see in himself a new attitude toward his father, which is described by Christians as "regeneration," becoming in a new way the son of your father, a "new birth" which means much more than the physical accident that you are his son.

LIFE'S PILGRIMAGE

That is quite enough about the United States.

Our parable bears some slight resemblance to the story of the Prodigal Son, but it is even more like a much older story, the story of the Exodus. That story is in the Bible for many purposes, but one of these is that we may have a picture of life's pilgrimage. It is a very good picture indeed. The place from which Israel came out, Egypt, is a place of bondage, but it was not until Moses arose among them that they realized how grievous and disastrous a bondage it was. They were persuaded that they must get away from Egypt, and take their journey toward a place where they could walk freely with their God. The journey took them forty years, and included every kind of experience of doubt, despair, and rebellion. Many times they said, "Why did you ever bring us here? We were better off under the Pharaohs." But in the end, at great cost, the journey was accomplished. Although it may have been to the outward eye little more than a mass migration, of interest mainly to specialists in ancient cultures, to Israel it was always symbolic of a "rescue," and of a "sanctifying" journey on which they were made aware of God's everlasting mercy, of their own abysmal inefficiency and need, and of the reality of God's promises. Israel's "conversion," you might say, dated from the moment Moses persuaded them first that they must make for the Promised Land. But at what cost their sanctification was wrought!

Life is that shape. Christians believe that God *is*, and that God is love. That means believing that God wants the love and trust of mankind. They believe that God has a goal for us all, and that this life is, or ought to be, a pilgrimage toward that goal, containing both evidences that point us to it, and disciplines that fit us to achieve it. "Nashville" is, if you like, heaven, but not merely in the sense that heaven is where you go when you are dead. It is also what the Fourth Gospel calls "eternal life," which starts here and now. It is the state of being "in God's confidence," or, in the grand Old Testament phrase, "walking with God" (Gen. 5:22, 24; 6:9; 24:40; Ps. 116:9; Mic. 6:8), or of being a "friend of God" (Isa. 41:8, Jas. 2:23).

Conversion is being put on that road, being started on the journey that leads from a conviction of God's contempt to a conviction of God's friendship. Regeneration is the slow and hazardous process of becoming reconciled in your own heart, and coming to believe in a God who wants this reconciliation and works for it. Sanctification is what the adventures of the road do for you to make you fit for the goal.

"ONCE-BORN" AND "TWICE-BORN"

Before we go further, there are two more things to say. One is to answer the common question, "What does it mean when people distinguish between the 'once-born' and the 'twice-born'?" The answer begins with a caution. "Twice-born" means, of course, born in the ordinary physical sense *plus* reborn in the spiritual sense we have just been attending to. In that sense every converted man is twice-born. But to some people the moment when they were set on the road is identifiable, and the moment when they began to think of their Father as their friend is identifiable; to others it is not. Remember that our parable is only one kind of story. There are other ways of getting to Nashville. There may have been (we allowed for this) no real conviction in the traveler's mind that his father despised him or had forgotten him, it may have been simply a matter of asking the way. He might have been walking the right way, and have been told by the stranger, "Keep straight on." It must be remembered that conversion—getting the traveler on the right road—might involve the correction of a selection of errors from an enormous number of possible errors on his part; it might involve a long journey from the wrong road to the right one, or a short one. It might be spread over a long period, here one flash of light, here another, adding up to a conversion that was perfectly authentic, but whose decisive moment would be impossible to determine. There is a very broad way of classifying people into those who can and those who cannot pinpoint their conversion by reference to a certain identifiable experience. The distinction is in the end artificial. Large allowance must always be made for those people who are fortunate enough never to have felt at all strongly that God was their enemy. Nobody *starts from* Nashville. Everybody must make a journey to get there. But it is a serious matter to say or imply that everybody's journey is from the same place, or begun by the same kind of cause. Between the man who clearly remembers the time when he thought his father was against him and the man who can remember no such period is a large area within which you can find conversions of every conceivable shape and size. Avoid this kind of hard and fast classification; it does nobody any good nowadays. But remember that whoever we are, and however happy and godly was our childhood, there is a journey for us to make; the one thing that is fatal is to live from one year's end to the next without learning anything new about our Father's love.

The other large matter is this. The Gospels are written to provide us with all the evidence we require both about the love of our Father for us and about how we must meet life's disciplines. There is so much to learn about what the love of God really means that we need the Gospels—all four of them—with their highly concentrated instruction and inspiration to guide us. Remember, however, that the Gospels are not there primarily to give us information, for interest's sake. They are there primarily to tell us who Jesus is, what manner of Person he is, and therefore what manner of Person is our Father. Our parable was wholly humanistic. Jesus was not in it. But put Jesus into it, let him be the Stranger, and let him be the Evidence. Then the story becomes at once a New Testament story, and we can press on.

THE AIM OF CONVERSION

Let us now say a little more about the destination, or the aim of conversion. Toward what is a man converted?

The commonest expression used of a man converted is to say that he has accepted Jesus Christ as "his Lord and Savior." In that expression there is nothing to quarrel with, but if that is an expression you often hear, or often use, you may already be wondering why it has not appeared in my first chapter. The answer to that is, I believe, of great importance.

To be honest, I do not myself believe that that expression means much to some people. To some it means everything, well and good. If that is what they mean, let them say it. But there are people whom I should regard as converted whose experience is not precisely described by those words. Therefore they need some explanation.

RECONCILIATION

The whole process of which conversion is a part is reconciliation. We have agreed on that. Reconciliation between whom? Between the traveler and his father, between the mortal man and his Father in heaven. "God was in Christ reconciling the world to himself." That is the Bible's expression (II Cor. 5:19). "God and sinners reconciled," says the familiar hymn. Not, you will observe, "Christ and sinners reconciled."

Reconciliation implies a separation, and what we are implying is a separation between mankind (including the traveler) and God. We are implying the separation between mankind and the whole of God—the Father, the Son, and the Holy Spirit. This separation is depicted in the Bible by the Old Testament rebellions against the revealed Law of God, by the violent and hateful rejection of Christ in the Gospels, and by the evidences in the New Testament of all those errors and ignorances by which we "grieve the Holy Spirit of God." What is looked for at the end of the road is a reconciliation involving not only Jesus Christ, but the whole mysterious and mighty personality of the living God.

We believe that God is the Maker of heaven and earth, of all things visible and invisible, that he is the Redeemer of the world in Jesus Christ, and that he is the Sanctifier and Sustainer of the world through the Holy Spirit. It is the whole of that Person with whom humanity is at odds. The understanding of and acceptance of Jesus Christ is in itself an enormous thing, but even that is not the whole story.

The way the Bible puts it seems to be roughly this. God created the world in love, through reason (Rev. 4:11; Prov. 8:22; John 1:3). God so created the world that mankind could love him; and that involved his so creating it that man could willfully neglect him and hate him, since love cannot be enslaved. ("In our image" [Gen. 1:26] cannot mean less than this.) Man went wrong, misusing the freedom that God gave him (Genesis 3). Man decided to regard the ordinances of God as vexatious and meaningless commands (Gen. 2:16-17; Ps. 81:11-12), although God had designed every one of them to be a pointer toward the technique of loving obedience that he wanted mankind to learn (Exod. 20:20). Thereafter you have this terrible situation with God and man at cross purposes—God extending love, and keeping in being all the ordinances that are designed to help us return that love (Matt. 5:18), and man insisting that God is a tyrant who bullies us and pushes us around, who is always angry, and who makes for us a world in which our life is likely to be spared only if we keep out of his way. It is all in the allegory of Eden, God seeking, man hiding, all the resentment and grievance in their situation having its origin in man's self-regard.

It was this situation that God sought to remedy through his various self-revelations—in law, in prophecy, in inspired writing; and it was in relation to this situation that he finally declared himself in Jesus Christ.

Now the vital point is this: our traveler, before he meets the stranger, is living in Eden after the Fall. He is not yet living in Christ's kingdom. He is still obstinately convinced that his father doesn't like him and doesn't want him.

LAW AND GRIEVANCE

And even if that is not an accurate statement about every individual man, it is a very fair description of the collective state of the world. Take the ordinary physical laws which govern the world. I ought to say that the philosophers raise questions about the rightness of the expression "laws of nature," but their point is not the same as mine here. I mean the law that says, in a general way, that if you jump off a skyscraper you will break your neck on the pavement below, or that if you do not attend to the drains you will get typhoid, or that if you overeat you will get fat and raise your blood pressure. All these laws are part of creation, and we know quite well that while some of them are easy enough to understand, and their "penalties" are easy enough to avoid (don't jump off the skyscraper), some have required a good deal of searching to reveal their nature (like the one about drains), and others need a certain amount of moral discipline if the consequences of their breach are to be avoided (eat less).

But now consider this: there is a large difference between the healthy man and the man who "takes care of his health." Many people, especially in our highly sophisticated civilization, live in a state of constant fear about their health. Their attitude toward the number of things that can go wrong is that there is a vast bureaucracy of incomprehensible laws governing the principles of health which they can't hope to keep up with, but which impose on them ceaseless exactions. There is a god of health whom they must placate, but how they hate him, and how they resent the way he hides his principles from them, and how much easier it would be if there were no ordinances at all!

The healthy man, of course, is the man who never thinks about his health, but who just does not want to do the things that bring bad health as their consequence, and gets into the habit of doing the things that keep health steady. It is not that he is always looking up the rules and deciding what to do. It is that he *likes* doing what brings good health, and does it without strain or a sense of being oppressed by duty.

Many people—most people, perhaps—take this line about the moral ordinances of God. Moral diseases of personality and society follow certain lines of action and decision as surely as typhoid follows bad drains—we know this. But most of us regard the moral law as a troublesome and exacting affair, without which the world would be much easier to live in. Why not commit adultery? Why not, when the shoe really pinches, steal? Why not chisel on the income-tax return?

Well, here is one man who avoids all these things, who lives as upright a life as he can, and who is always taking care that you know it. He makes a great labor of it all, and does not enjoy a moment of it. Here is another man, whose life is just as upright and law-abiding, and who yet seems to be made happier, not less happy, by doing right. It does not seem to occur to him to regard the moral law as vexatious. So his energy is set free for all kinds of gracious acts which make you say not "What a good man that is," but, "What a lovable man that is."

The pattern is the same through the whole texture of causes and consequences which govern life. Is it conceivable that Mozart looked up all the rules of music before he wrote a bar? Did he live, as a musician, in fear of or under bondage to music's law? Is it not more reasonable to say that he had achieved that state in which the last thing he wanted to do was break the laws of music, and all his energy was set free to make music as eloquent and beautiful as it could be made?

What is the difference between the mechanic who nurses his machine, and him who bullies it, treating it as his enemy? What is the difference between the farmer who nurses his land, exercising friendly dominion over it, and the farmer who, regarding all nature as a conspiracy to starve him, starves and browbeats his land until it is sterile? What is the difference between the man who has suffered a crushing blow and thereafter sees that an account is sent in to all his neighbors in terms of selfishness and egocentricity, and the man who suffering a similar blow says, "Now, what good action has this made it easier for me to do for my neighbor's sake?"

The difference, in every case, is between the reconciled and the unreconciled mind. Reconciliation and its techniques repeat themselves all over the pattern.

RECONCILIATION WITH THE FATHER

Reconciliation on the scale we are handling it in this book is a total reconciliation of man with his Father in heaven, a total setting aside of all those thoughts of the Father's hostility that may have made man feel like a smart fellow for outwitting the Father, but that are the source of all his worst distresses. This leads to the condition in which what the Father wants, man wants; he is delivered from the state in which what the Father wants, he resentfully accepts. The whole of the world is to be reconciled with the whole of God; it is not merely a moral reconciliation or a "spiritual" reconciliation, whatever that might be. It is a total relation of love. A personal conversion is the kind of process that fits into, and reflects on its own scale, this pattern. The fact that it has its physical aspects is adequately attested by the great prominence given in the Gospels to works of healing.

THE PATTERN OF CHRIST'S LIFE

Look at the life of Jesus. His life was a pattern of the fully reconciled life. Jesus was entirely healthy, physically perfect through all life's natural changes. But Jesus was no hypochondriac, taking care of his health. Jesus was "tempted like as we are," but never made a wrong moral decision. The account in the Gospels of his encounters with temptation, if carefully read, does not suggest that he found temptation attractive, or that he wanted to do what his Father forbade. On the contrary, it is clear that he found it loathsome, and that the pressure of this loathsome thing upon his perfect goodness was the cause of the pain of his temptation. He *wanted* to do God's will.

Jesus had the mastery over nature, and his mastery tells us two important things. It tells us first that we ought not to be too sure that we are utterly at the mercy of the blind forces of a hostile creation—germs, earthquakes, volcanoes, forest fires. We ought to consider how many of our sicknesses are caused by our attitude toward things and people, our fears, anxieties, and laziness; we ought to consider how many of our natural disasters represent forces with which we should attempt to come to terms, rather than forces which are inexorably hostile to us. We need not, perhaps, be so comfortably— or desperately—fatalistic about these things as is our habit.

But, secondly, Jesus' mastery over nature, as manifested in his miracles, is always recorded by the evangelists in order to tell us something about faith, and something about God, to show God's concern and horror over the malformations of natural life, to show that a certain kind of helplessness on our part is something we must put away, especially when it is born of grievance, and to show us that what we must do is to stop grumbling about life's inconveniences and troubles, and face them on the assumption that God is for us, not against us. (It can all be read, for example, in John 5, especially verses 7 and 14, where it is made clear that the object of this miracle, and of all miracles, is not primarily the removal of an inconvenience or distress, but the bringing to life of a healthy and cheerful relation between man and God.)

The Gospels give us the pattern of the life toward which a man is "turned" when he is converted. The life of Jesus gives us that pattern in every possible dimension. If I have here given the impression that to frame a doctrine of conversion in sectional terms, or in technically religious terms, or in merely "spiritual" terms, is on the whole a dangerous thing to do, and that I regard it as better to think of conversion as leading to "friendship with God," that is the impression I wanted to give. As we go on, we can amplify this.

WHO CONVERTS?

When a man is converted, who converts him?

There is only one way to answer this question, and that is by calling in the philosophers to help us. We are after the real cause of a man's conversion, and we must find out what we mean by "cause."

Take a secular example. When I switch on the light in my study, what is the cause of the appearance of light in the room? There are dozens of answers. Here are some: the glowing of an incandescent filament in the bulb; the completion of an electrical circuit by my snapping a switch; myself, who snapped the switch; my desire to get a book from the shelf; the power station that supplies the electricity; my wife, who asked for the book. . . .

In one line you can take it all back to the creation of the world by way of the ancient vegetation that made the coal that fires the furnaces in the power station. In another line you can take it back to the Creator through a chain of motives. In another you can take it forward to him by a chain of purposes. It all depends where you want to stop. Are you saying, "Who turned on that light?" or are you saying, "What makes a light bulb glow?" or are you being very high-minded and saying, "What is the explanation of all these wonders that we take for granted in our daily lives?" or is it simply, "Why did you turn on that light?"

Now in a man's conversion there are as many causes as there are in any other event of mortal life. Primarily, the cause is God. Finally, the cause is God. But it is always important to keep in view the fact that God *always*—not only in secular affairs, but always—acts in the world through secondary causes. That is to say, when God wills that this or that shall happen, he effects the operation through things or people, and it is right to describe these as causes. Indeed, when it is people with whom you are dealing, as it is here, it is right to regard them as free agents and wrong to call them blind, insensitive instruments. You use a hammer to drive in a nail. The hammer is hardly at all to be thought of as the cause of the nail's being driven in. But God does not use anything, least of all people, in the way you used that hammer. To God no person is ever an instrument, or a hand, or a unit; what is more, to God nothing is ever merely a thing.

People sometimes talk as if there were only a few kinds of people and things that God can use as collaborators in the work of conversion. That is wrong. God—and it is God the Holy Spirit of whom we speak here—can use anybody or anything for that purpose.

CLASSIC CONVERSIONS

It happens that certain very well-known conversions have been dramatically described and decisively worked, and we think of them as being the only kind, or the only genuine kind, of conversion. There is Paul the apostle, for example. His conversion, as recorded in Acts 9, was effected by an encounter with the risen

Christ. That was true conversion without any doubt. If ever anybody said, "Stop, attend, and turn about," it was Jesus to Paul on that day. Yet you cannot say that this conversion is the only kind that anybody may expect.

What is more, you cannot say either that it was unprepared (How much had Stephen to do with it? How much had Paul's pharisaic training to do with it?) or that it was entirely finished with that encounter (What happened in the fourteen years between that moment and the exceedingly interesting conversation recorded in Gal. 2:1-14?). All manner of factors besides the decisive encounter can be called causes of that conversion.

There is St. Augustine, who was converted by reading a passage of Scripture. His attention was drawn to it by his overhearing a child next door, perhaps in the course of some child's game, saying over and over again, "Take and read. Take and read." Augustine tells us quite clearly that the cause of it all was God, the Holy Spirit, but his *Confessions,* which neither begin nor end with this decisive incident, are written to show how God strung on a continuous line of cause and effect all manner of events which otherwise might have seemed to be isolated accidents.

There is John Wesley, who was converted—not from contempt of Christ to love of Christ, but from a conventional and ineffective faith to a blazing fire of faith—by hearing a sermon based on Luther's *Commentary on Romans.* Earlier in the day he had heard the choir of St. Paul's, London, singing an anthem setting of Psalm 130. How much had that, and how much had his frustrating years in Georgia and his Oxford fellowship, to do with his conversion?

Paul (in Acts 22 and 26), Augustine, and Wesley all tell of their conversions as Jeremiah does in his first chapter. It is always, "I hardly knew at the time, but now I see how it was all working out." And if in Paul's case we must concede that the conversion was, compared with the others, achieved with remarkable completeness in a short space, we must also concede that an encounter with the Risen Christ is in any case a historical experience which has not been, in that precise manner, repeated since, and which plays no part in these other conversions.

PREDESTINATION?

Now is it right to say that conversions are divinely predestined? It is right, if we interpret rightly that somewhat sinister word. Converted men agree in saying that, as they now see it, nothing that went before their conversion was an accident, that everything, including their earlier hesitations and rebellions and wanderings and protests against Christ, was part of the pattern. But they did not know this at the time. At the time they were perfectly free agents. It is only now that they see the pattern. Now consider: what agency is capable of making a discernible pattern out of a man's life, while at every point it leaves him free and never enslaves him? Whose work is marked out from all other operations by that special and unique faculty of leaving free and yet working a pattern? Why, the only such agent is God, the Holy Spirit. Nobody else acts like that. Our traveler left Chicago by a free choice, turned toward Nashville by a free acceptance of persuasion, he wasn't kidnapped. But once on the way, he would say in his best moments,

"Why, everything led to this. Suppose I had decided to go to Los Angeles! What good fortune!"

Or put it another way. The man who met him and put him on the road to his father's house was, as it were, a very important agent in his conversion. But he was not the only agent. What is more, he cannot be absolutely sure that the traveler will ever complete his journey. He cannot himself ensure that he does. Indeed, if he insisted on accompanying the traveler all the way, he would probably be exercising, whether or not he meant to do so, a measure of coercion which would actually deprive the traveler of the full benefits of reconciliation. He might chatter so much as to leave the traveler no time to think things out for himself. He might, with misplaced benevolence, shield him from some of the disciplines of free choice, and so leave part of his spirit undeveloped. No, the stranger must leave him and trust that he will meet other people at the right moments who will help him and then themselves leave him. The traveler must encounter a series of persuasions that demand free assent, and give that assent, and press on from one to the next. It all gets more and more like the *Pilgrim's Progress*, though, come to think of it, it is even more like C. S. Lewis' *Pilgrim's Regress*, which is, perhaps, more attuned to the modern mind, and which you should certainly not miss.

The persuasions that accompany sanctification, and the preparatory causes of conversion, may be of any kind whatever. It all depends on what kind of person the subject of conversion is. For some, the most memorable moment will be an experience in church (like Isaiah 6). For others it will be the effect of a friend's character.

For others again, it will be an evangelical mission. For others—and let religious activists never forget this—it may be a book, and not necessarily the Bible. The most manifest case of conversion in my personal experience—Christian background, formal and lapsed Christianity evoking conscious rebellion, then the flash of saving light —came to a person from reading a book by Charles Williams. Why not? Nothing whatever is disqualified from being an instrument of the Holy Spirit in his work of conversion. Anything may shock a person into going back and taking the road toward Christ's kingdom.

The classic examples—Paul, Augustine, Wesley, and people of that kind—are not always helpful. They may be a positive danger. People who write books that hammer away at that kind of dramatic religious conversion can do a great deal of damage. There are plenty of religious people today who are driven half-frantic by the conviction that they have not been converted simply because they can find nothing in their past lives to correspond to the Damascus Road. There won't be. You are you, and not Paul or Augustine or Wesley. You could hear Luther on Romans and be bored stiff. The book that converted Charles Wesley, Luther's *Commentary on Galatians,* did bore John Wesley stiff. It is much more likely that if you are able to take time off to reflect on these matters, and if you value your religion highly enough, you will be able to recognize in your past life a number of "great moments," none of which is obviously decisive, but all of which are marked by some kind of illumination, some new thing learned about God in Christ. One thing is certain—if you are on the right road—and that is that you will never dream of taking any credit for your conversion. You will say, "How lucky I have been!" And that is the way to think of pre-destination.

"I FAILED TO CONVERT HIM"

There is one question which a pastor occasionally hears, and hears with great sorrow. It might be in this form. "I tried hard to convert my husband; I failed, and he died. It may be my fault that he has gone to hell. Can you help me?"

The answer to that begins here: "He hasn't gone to hell. If he has, it is not you who have sent him there. In this life each of us must make a decision affecting eternal life. But we must remember that, in the end, God's judgment determines everything (I Cor. 4:5). While *you* were there you were almost certainly helping him not to make the wrong choice. What happens in this life may make it more likely, or less likely, that a man will make his final decision. But you cannot send another person to hell, however close to him you have been. The worst you can do is to 'cause him to stumble,' to make it more difficult for him to see his way to heaven.

"Well, have you done that? If you claim that you have never done so, you're a better person than I am. We all do it. Some people are not hurt by it as much as others. But what was your intention? You really wanted, more than anything else, that he should find God? Then go in peace. God forgives sins. God forgives everything except the sin of not wanting forgiveness. You want forgiveness, for yourself and for him. We will pray for it together, and you will get it. Remember, God loves him and is showing him at this moment things that you and I couldn't show him. What you said and did may have looked as if it was falling on stony ground. But it is now bearing fruit you have never dreamed of."

What can be done to help conversion must be done. It is a terrible thing to place a log across an innocent man's road, so that he cannot help tripping over it (Matt. 18:6). Teachings, attitudes, habits that keep people off the road are an abomination, and they are very freely practiced by people and by society. They must be constantly rebuked. But here is the great comfort—that conversion is the Holy Spirit's work, and that it is not finished in this life. It is the Holy Spirit's very special work (Romans 8) to make sense of our sinful, selfish, and halting prayers, and to overrule for good our fumbling, clumsy actions.

THE EFFECTS OF CONVERSION

We come now to a very hazardous subject. The question behind what I write here is primarily, "How do I know if I am converted?" There is, of course, the related question, "How do I know if my neighbor is converted?" Here, I say, we are in great peril.

What we all want to say, of course, is, "If you're converted, you'll be like me." And the real trap there is that it is not in itself a wrong or wicked thing to say. Everybody agrees that there was something infectious and dynamic about the faith of the apostle Paul. Well, Paul said at Agrippa's court, "I would to God that not only you but also all who hear me this day might become such as I am—except for these chains"; and he wrote to the Corinthians twice, "be imitators of me" (I Cor. 4:16; 11:1), though in the second of those places he significantly adds, "as I am of Christ."

You go to the Rockies for the first time after spending, say, the first forty years of your life in New York City. You come back telling everybody about it. You show your color slides and tell your stories. You sound as if you had bought the Rockies. There's nothing like the Rockies, and they're all yours, and everybody else must come and see them. Why not? You have had a personal experience, and they really are "yours" in a way they were not before. There is nothing very unnatural in your enthusiasm. But always look out for the quiet fellow who talks around the stem of his pipe and says, "Sure, brother, I'll go to the Rockies. But not with you."

This is pushing me into my fifth chapter before I have written this one. What matters here is to notice in how many senses "be like me" may turn out to be the wrong, or the inexpedient, thing to say. Some religiously enthusiastic people spend much time saying, "Come and see what the Lord has done for my soul," and although there is nothing unnatural or hypocritical about this, they frequently fail to allow for comments from their hearers, usually unexpressed, which would surprise and sadden them. Don't insist on taking people to heaven in your own personal Cadillac.

Taking the matter quite generally, we might expect the most evident effects of conversion to be moral effects. And it is surely safe to say that if a man claims to have been converted, but lives a life that is at any point grossly and habitually immoral, his claim is unacceptable. That might seem to be a point almost too obvious to be worth making, except that people so easily forget the wider connotations of the word "immoral." It is as impossible to reconcile a claim to conversion with a life of habitual greed or dishonesty or covetousness or vanity or sloth or ill temper as it is to reconcile it with a life of habitual fornication. While too much is sometimes made by the zealous of the distinction between the "outwardly religious" and the "converted," it is obvious that a man who appears to do his outward duty by the church and who in business adopts a settled policy of acquisitiveness and meanness has missed the essential point of conversion. We need say little more about that.

"HABITUAL RIGHTEOUSNESS"

But I think it is important to draw special attention to those words, "habitual" and "settled." It is quite wrong to suppose that a converted man is incapable of lapses. Of course he is capable of them. He is tempted, and he falls. Yet there is much practical wisdom in the old tag in Proverbs (24:16), "A righteous man falls seven times, and rises again; but the wicked are overthrown by calamity." That sentence distinguishes between the man who is *habitually* turned toward God, which is what *righteous* means when it is used of men, and him who is *habitually* turned away from God.

It corresponds very well with life. Here are two people who are convicted of the same offense—say, of falsifying an income-tax return. It is proved against them. In neither case is it a genuine oversight; they meant to do it. It is a form of avarice, and legally punishable. But, as a matter of fact, you know perfectly well that in one of those men it is a lapse from a life of normally good conduct, that he will pay up and not commit the offense again; while in the other case it is part of a settled policy of swindling, and he has every intention of doing it again if he can bring it off without being detected. Of the first man you say, "He shouldn't have done that," but twelve months later you have forgotten about it; while of the second you say, "I am not surprised. He is that kind of man." 2017740

That is an analogy which is designed to lead from a familiar distinction between people of settled antisocial habit and people of settled good conduct to the religious distinction between people habitually turned toward God and people habitually turned against him. There is a difference between the man who falls into sin, and yet respects God and accepts God's judgment, and the man who sins in open contempt of God. There is no difference between the sins, but there is a difference between the men.

Conversion implies the beginning of a settled habit of life. Sanctification is the process of making that settled habit really settled, of establishing a God-centered equilibrium, and it takes time. You might say that that is what time is for—to accommodate the *process* of sanctification.

This settled habit, which includes the physical, the moral, and the spiritual faculties of a man, is settled in both the new and the old senses of that word. It really is a habit; there really is an equilibrium that is beginning to become stable. But also "settled" implies that about this person there is a special and unmistakable kind of *peace*. "Thou dost keep him in perfect peace, whose mind is stayed on thee" (Isa. 26:3) is not merely an anthem with an agreeable tune, it is the soundest possible psychology.

ANXIETY

No psychologist has ever succeeded in explaining religion away. On the contrary, psychology has given us several new words of which religious thought can make very good use. The one that comes in useful here is "anxiety."

Anxiety is the state of mind our traveler was beginning to experience during his last few months in Chicago, and which he experienced much more when he had been a few days on the road. It is the best possible description of the state of mind we have already ascribed to mankind in its post-Fall, pre-Christian situation. Anxiety can be innocent or guilty. It comes from insecurity. The youngster emerging from the security of home begins to feel it, and it is right that he should, because it drives him out to make his own life. But the worst side of it is where he feels that his father dislikes him. Mankind is, in its unredeemed state, sure that God despises it. The consequence of this is a dangerous anxiety that makes mankind truculent and aggressive and selfish. It is like the condition of the unwanted child. There on the couch in the psychiatrist clinic the patient peels off layer after layer of blissful forgetfulness until at last he has exposed what he had forgotten — his unhappy childhood, some quarrel between his parents, a divorce, or something else that rocked his world to its foundations. The psychologist diagnoses an anxiety.

The Christian diagnoses an anxiety in a world that has lost its Father; the only difference here is that the Father has contributed nothing to its cause. There is no divorce, no gesture of contempt toward the child. So the anxiety is one of guilt, because the state of affairs that has developed cannot be anybody else's fault. But guilt makes for just as much insecurity as grievance does, and insecurity is the chief characteristic of the fallen world. It is no help to say to that world, "It is your fault. Put it right." Only God in his grace and generosity can do that.

At the personal level, this insecurity makes itself evident in the ways that psychology has led us to expect. What evidences do we usually have for neurotic and psychotic conditions? What makes us rush people off to the doctor and the sanitarium? Always, some kind of antisocial tendency or behavior. Anything from habitual moroseness to murder can be a symptom of this anxiety. And the life from which men are converted is a life whose chief evidences are things hardly less diverse or terrible. There is a moroseness directed against whatever it is that is running the universe. There is a fatalistic fear of displeasing some deity of luck. There is a settled grievance against the shortcomings of a man's neighbors. There is a certainty that the world of men and things is a conspiracy to do him down, and a corresponding attitude toward men and things of defensiveness, suspicion, and hostility.

That is the state of affairs with which God had to deal; and he dealt with it in the life, passion, and resurrection of Christ. Rescue work was required, and rescue work was done, for which the Christian word, we remember, is "salvation."

But, of course, rescue work is not enough for a situation like that. To have brought mankind out of the slavery of fear is one thing, but the positive replacement of that fear by love is another. It was necessary for God so to present himself to man that man could see not only that God is strong enough to rescue him, but that he values man enough to want him and respect him.

THE HUMILITY OF GOD'S FORGIVENESS

There is too little in modern presentations of the Christian religion that stresses this enormous fact. God is too frequently presented as one who rescues, but then treats the rescued man with highhanded patronage, making what preachers have sometimes actually called "totalitarian" demands on him. "I've got you out of the mess. Now you'll do what I say"—that kind of thing. But that is not at all what happens.

If I had a friend who had got into grievous trouble through his own fault, and had made away with other people's money including some of mine, I might go and pay his debts for him, and set him up in business, and underwrite him for the first five years, and so forth; but I doubt if I should be able to resist the temptation to call the tune, to insist on his remaining under a sense of obligation to me. I might free him from one slavery, but I doubt if I am big enough not to substitute for it another, a moral slavery to me and my money and power. (That is why it is often said that it is our benefactors whom we hate the most.) But God is not like that. Is the character of Christ, as displayed in the Gospels, like that?

What the Gospels tell us is that God saved man by treating him with an incredible and absolutely undeserved *respect*. The most revealing sentence about this in all Scripture is in one of our Lord's parables (Mark 12:6): "They will respect my son." The words are put into the mouth of the owner of the vineyard whose tenants had treated it so badly. "They will respect my son." They did nothing of the kind. They murdered him. Nonetheless, they must be treated as though they would. (The sense of the terrible words about destruction which close that parable is undoubtedly, "Ought not God to do this?" The really frightening thing is that God will not, and has not.) In Isa. 63:8 the prophet puts similar words into God's mouth: "Surely they are my people, sons who will not deal falsely." It goes on, "So he became their Savior"—*so*, because of that, and by that technique, he became their rescuer. So God lived our life, took our flesh, put himself into our hands, and trusted us with this treasure. In the act of dying, Jesus manifested this terrible love of God, this inconceivable respect and "courtesy" of God, and in his resurrection he showed that it is that love, and not any corrupt worldly power or force, that makes the world go round, that *that*, not hostile, fear-ridden bullying, is the first principle of the universe.

ASSURANCE

I venture to say, then, that in the converted man you may expect to see some symptom of this assurance of being wanted by God. It may show itself in all manner of ways. It is likely to issue in a character singularly free from vanity and pride. If your standing with God is what Christ's cross and resurrection proclaim it to be, what need is there of defensiveness? In conversation unegotistical, in business generous without imprudence or foolishness which might infringe on others' rights as much as acquisitiveness would have done—such a man regards his health, his sanity, his religion not as things hardly won and jealously to be guarded, but as things freely and undeservedly given, to be used for others' good.

How do I know whether I am converted? I think that in the end the clue is here. Are you primarily concerned with winning points over a hostile universe? Or when your mind wanders freely, does it normally fasten either on your neighbors or on Jesus Christ and the glory of God? It is a matter of equilibrium and settled habit. Prayer can achieve it. It can be given, but not striven for. But I dare to say that whether or not you go to church, whether or not you commonly talk about salvation and the state of your soul, whether your favorite reading is detective stories or sermons, if you do know what it is to be at peace without being callous, to be free without being presumptuous, to enjoy other people for their sakes and to enjoy the truth for its sake, to forget for long periods the question, "What do I get out of this," then you know quite a lot about what conversion is.

EVANGELISM

Evangelism is the process by which the gospel is preached to men from one generation to another. "Evangel" means "good news," and "gospel" is an old Saxon word meaning the same thing. The good news is that God wants men and loves them, and it is always news, and always good. Does this world look as though it knew that its Creator loves it? Does it look as though it knew that its Creator is good?

There are two ways of looking at the church's task of evangelism. One is to say that the church in its day-by-day ministry does nothing else, that the traditional rites of the church, together with faithful preaching, are the evangelical activity of the Holy Spirit. The other is to treat any age as one in which ambulance work must be performed, in which the routine of the church must be supplemented by what is usually called "revival." When that second conviction takes hold of people, we not infrequently see groups pressing for revival outside the church's traditional scheme. This happened especially in the thirteenth, sixteenth, and eighteenth centuries in Europe, and is happening to an unprecedented extent now. Associated with such movements is a conviction here and there that it is not the supplementing of the church's traditional techniques by revival that is wanted, but their replacement by it. That is a view which I believe to be misconceived, understandable though it be.

43

Either kind of evangelism is directed toward conversion. It should not be overlooked by enthusiasts for revivalism that the church's liturgies have always been designed toward conversion and sanctification; preaching is the primary agent, within the traditional scheme, of conversion, and the sacraments of sanctification.

Two texts, apparently contradictory, present themselves to my mind as I write this. One is in Luke 9:49-50: "John answered, 'Master, we saw a man casting out demons in your name, and we forbade him, because he does not follow with us.' But Jesus said to him, 'Do not forbid him; for he that is not against you is for you.'" The other is two pages further on, Luke 11:23: "He who is not with me is against me, and he who does not gather with me scatters." It seems fairly clear that the first text rebukes needless religious sectarianism, and that the second rebukes all manner of secular demagogy. The upshot seems to be that disagreement with *you*, with *your* conception of Christ is no ground for denouncing somebody else as a false evangelist, but disagreement with Christ, misrepresentation of his teaching, gathering a large following by replacing his teaching with something else places any leader in grave danger. In any case, it is not we but Christ who is the judge; not our standards but his must be the measure of the judgment.

That said, it seems right to make two comments on the techniques of evangelism which seem to be supported by the evidence of the Scriptures.

LORDSHIP TRUE AND FALSE

The first is that the gospel should not be presented as an enslaving claim. It is often difficult to do otherwise, when one talks of the total lordship of Christ. But it must always be remembered that Christ refused as a temptation of the devil any kind of lordship as the world understands it. He would not let them make him king (John 6:15). He contrasted the world's lordship with lordship in the kingdom (Mark 10:42-44), leaving us in no doubt that his own lordship is that of service, which means respect to others, not contempt for their freedom. Most impressively of all, he said when on trial before Pilate that his kingdom is "not of this world; if my kingship were of this world, my servants would fight" (John 18:36). Therefore in techniques of evangelism that which is of this world's power, whether it suggests physical power or psychological power, must always be suspected of partaking of that "lordship" which the Master set aside. Modern men glibly criticize the physical power of the medieval Inquisition; we must not be less wary of the psychological power techniques of certain kinds of modern evangelism. Physical and psychological power are combined in mass techniques, and in the supervision of all enterprises which employ them ceaseless vigilance is of first importance.

It must be recognized that the desire for a certain kind of influence may be a corrupt desire, and it is worth our while to ponder whether in the long run the renunciation of wide influence may not be as potent a factor in the spreading of the gospel as its acceptance. It may look like burying a talent. It may involve a man in the charge of being lazy or complacent or incompetent. It will not be recognized by many for sanctity. But history tells us of many obscure saints—and history has forgotten many more—who have been powerful agents for lasting conversion in a manner denied to the popular and eminent.

The necessity of saying this is borne in on me by the fact that while in these days of easy communication many names of influential men of religion are well known to us all, and not a word would I say against the sanctity of any of them, I can in fact think of only one example in my own country of a man who deliberately renounced wide religious influence. He became in the early forties a religious leader of enormous popularity, drawing crowds wherever he spoke and selling religious books by the hundreds of thousands, who quite soon turned his back on the career of religious eminence that had opened before him, devoting himself instead to the faithful performance of his professional work and to numberless private works of charity. His name I will not mention, because to do so would frustrate his own purpose, but many of my readers would recognize it at once if I did so.

THE DELUSION OF CONFORMITY

Secondly, it is almost certainly wrong to represent conversion as a mere conformity. It is wrong to give the impression that every traveler takes the same road. If in any evangelistic enterprise the convert is made to feel that he is required to conform uncritically to some man-made system, though it be adorned with the trappings of piety, it is likely that he is being deceived about the true nature of conversion.

It is a dangerous sign when personal criticism is silenced by an evangelist, at whatever level it may be offered. Certain evangelistic bodies display a singular, and surely unevangelical, tendency to disregard criticism, and to take the line that in matters religious they can do no wrong. The publication of many adulatory comments and no adverse ones in propaganda sheets is an accepted technique of the advertising world of commerce, but it has nothing to do with the gospel method.

Similarly, the softening up of the critical faculties of a congregation by the use of music specially designed for the purpose, or a decor that suggests extreme and ruthless efficiency, and perhaps of a massed choir that suggests the sheer weight of numbers (physical power) is morally questionable. The propagation of an attitude even to the Scriptures that treats them as a collection of magical incantations toward which no criticism may be directed is similarly deplorable. The building up of a single personality to the stature of a superman to whom the masses pay homage is disagreeably reminiscent of certain contemporary, and very ancient, political corruptions.

I think the best comment on evangelistic work comes from one of the most dangerously penetrating books that has been written these many years. It is *Mental Seduction and Menticide*, by the American psychologist, Dr. Joost A. M. Meerloo of Columbia; it is not a religious book, but it offers a diagnosis of the special diseases of our modern society. At one point its author writes: "In a totalitarian world, everybody is educated in self-denial and self-betrayal; when a person becomes a nonconformist, the label 'traitor' will be attached to him. In a world stifled by dogma and tradition, every form of original thinking may be called sedition and treason." My readers will know what secular civilization we commonly accuse of manifesting this dreadful vice, but is there nothing here of which the evangelists should not take note?

"Self-denial" is perhaps the key word. It is an ambiguity there that turns the whole business from blessing to cursing. Self-denial is a gospel word, a gospel demand, and it is an act of pure joy and courage. But none but Christ may demand it. If at any point a man demands it in his own right, he is scattering, not gathering. The very least coercion by a human agency, the very least loading of the dice or weighting of the scale or slanting of the evidence, taking advantage of a man's innocence, his suffering, his fear, his incapacity to reason quickly, his anxiety, is a crime against the person Christ died to claim for himself.

The evangelist ought to expect trouble from his converts. The gospel prevails against resistance—Thomas' resistance, or Peter's, or Paul's, or that of James and John. The gospel does not prevail by first using a psychological drug to extort a confession.

THE DELUSION OF CHEAPNESS

Thirdly, and it follows very obviously, evangelism that represents the benefits of the kingdom as obtainable quickly and cheaply is cruelly delusive. Here again, the exploitation of glamour is to be discouraged. King Saul was a "choice young man and goodly" (I Sam. 9:2), a head taller than anybody else. Compare the fruit of his labors (II Sam. 1:17-27) with his work of whom it is written, "He had no beauty that we should desire him"

(Isa. 53:2). Perfection is not glamorous. It is, at certain moments, frightening.

I have ventured to write elsewhere about the curious history and the doubtful merit of "revival music." Here I would say only that it is a conveniently complete example of that deliberate cheapening of the appurtenances of the gospel which can lead to and may proceed from a cheapening of the gospel itself. It is designed to induce in the would-be convert a sense of repose and security which is wholly at variance with the gospel as our Lord taught it, and as he worked it out in his life and death. No matter whether revival music may have at one period of history brought blessing to many, it is in our time, when the distresses which drove men to hear that great saint and genius, Sankey, are no longer with us, a positive impediment to the gospel. It should be very firmly excluded from public worship, and its banishment from evangelistic campaigns would be entirely for the best.

The object of all evangelism is conversion, and conversion is, in a sense, growing up. When the convert is compared to a child in the famous passage in Matthew 18, it should be remembered that every child always longs to grow up. "When I grow up, I'll be a truck driver." The kingdom does not extinguish that gallant ambition. It thrives on it. The kingdom is the only condition in which it can be really achieved. Growing up is costly. For those who watch the child developing through adolescence it is embarrassing and exasperating and a great trial to the patience. So is the business of conversion, and any evangelistic technique which seeks to keep men at the stage of childhood is an insult to them and to the gospel.

It can sometimes be done delusively, but it is done. It may be said by an evangelist, "Go and prosper. Be a flourishing businessman or a successful film star or whatever it is you want to be. God will help you if you keep his laws." Well and good, but if behind this it is implied, "But when you come here you'll do what you're told," if the convert is required to be a he-man outside church and a docile infant inside it, trouble will be round the corner.

TWO TEXTS

I end with two more difficult and searching texts. When Jesus had explained the parable of the sower, he said to his friends, "To you has been given the secret of the kingdom of God, but for those outside everything is in parables" (Mark 4:11). A terrifying text, but face it! It seems that our Lord, speaking to a generalized multitude, deliberately so spoke that there would be no doubt in their minds of the difficulty of approaching the kingdom. There was a certain kind of "simplicity," an i-dotting and t-crossing nursemaid fussiness, which he carefully avoided. Those who clamor for "simple" sermons are usually asking for addresses which will not rebuke them or demand that they take mental pains. They are conformists, and to encourage them is to drain all the life out of the kingdom. The gospel prevails against resistance in the believer, and presents to him not always a smiling face and a simple word. Those who present it must never overlook this, or their hearers will be later cruelly disappointed.

The other text is recorded at the return of the seventy (Luke 10:20). "Do not rejoice in this, that the spirits are subject to you; rejoice that your names are written in heaven." It is a great thing to see the citadel of unbelief falling before your eyes. But are you seeing what is there, or what you wish to see? The real work is done "in heaven," that is, by the Holy Spirit.

PRIVATE EVANGELISM

What God does, he may do by public evangelism, but he may also do it through private evangelism. How really do you get an unbeliever into the faith? By reasoning with him? Partly, but not wholly. By presenting the faith to him in a fresh and spectacular way? Possibly, but not wholly. By fraternal kindness? Maybe, but if all these fail, what is left? Why, to die for him.

For the sake of his faith, it may be his friend's privilege to kill in himself, to disregard utterly and throw away, some ambition, some plan, some desire—to give up your job, which you like and do well, and let him have it, to give up your right to leisure and wealth, to give up whatever you really cannot spare, and take the responsibility of seeing that you alone, and not your dependents, bear the burden. It might be any of those things. The disciple is not greater than his Master, but the Master did more than that for him. If you want to see costly evangelism, evangelism that pays no dividend at all in recognizable result, evangelism that must bear the burden of ingratitude or misunderstanding or lack of recognition, look every time at private evangelism. You will have a hard time finding an example because that kind of thing is done secretly by people who are disinclined to talk about it and who are interested in what is written in heaven. A suffering church, a suffering neighbor—these are the best agents of evangelism.

CONVERSION, FAITH, AND THE CHURCH

I hope that my reader is not too greatly disappointed that I have forborne to mention in my last chapter the name of any individual evangelist. Certain evangelists, with their teams or organizations, are so conspicuous just now that it would be natural to expect some comment on them. But to be critical of an organization or an institution thrusts us forward at once toward some consideration of what the church's place in the work of conversion is. What we must say here falls into two halves.

FAITH

In the first place, we must roundly state that conversion without faith is impossible. What then is faith? It is a God-given quality in the would-be convert. Once given, it is self-developing, but until it is there, nothing can happen (Matt. 13:58).

We must distinguish between faith as a quality of the man preparing for conversion, and faith as a quality of the converted man. Both qualities are expressed by the same word, but clearly there is a difference between them.

The best clue to its meaning in the first sense is in those places where our Lord recognizes and commends the faith of somebody who has come to him in great need. Consider the places in the Gospels where he is reported as saying "Your faith has saved you," or words to that effect. Of these there are eight:

1) the centurion's servant (Matt. 8:10; Luke 7:9)

2) the paralytic with his four friends (Matt. 9:2; Mark 2:5; Luke 5:20)

3) the ruler's daughter (Matt. 9:22)

4) the Syrophoenician (or Canaanite) woman (Matt. 15:28; Mark 7:29)

5) the woman with the issue of blood (Mark 5:34; Luke 8:48)

6) the blind man (Bartimaeus) (Mark 10:52; Luke 18:42)

7) the woman with the ointment whose sins were forgiven (Luke 7:50)

8) the Samaritan leper (Luke 17:19).

In all these cases you can observe three things: first, a condition of dire need; second, the admission of that need expressed in some act or statement that has clearly cost much; and, third, a clear indication that the sufferer knows that Christ, *and nobody else,* can help him. Case 1 expresses the need through the singular action of a highly placed officer of a heathen faith coming himself, and not sending some servant, to the Jewish Rabbi; case 3 is similar. In case 2 it is the persistence of the four friends that expresses it. In case 4 it is the obstinate, impudent, and altogether remarkable belief of a woman of foreign culture in the power of the Rabbi. In case 5 it is once again the persistence of the afflicted woman, together with her costly admission of an embarrassing physical condition, on which our Lord insists. In case 6 it is what amounts to a confession of faith in Jesus as the Messiah on the part of an obviously lively-witted and well-known blind man. In case 7 the costliness of the confession is symbolized in the value of the ointment and the daring of the woman in coming unannounced into a men's party. In case 8 it is in the gratitude of a leper who, being a Samaritan among Jews, is doubly afflicted and doubly in need. And in every case there is something here to correspond with the admission of the woman with the issue of blood that she has consulted every physician within reach, and that Jesus is positively her last chance. "If you let me down," they all say, "then indeed I am finished. But you will not."

It can surely be assumed that in those cases where Jesus was dealing with rational people, he looked always for something of this sort, even where he is not reported as having drawn attention to it. It can also be said with perfect safety that the Fourth Gospel does not report this kind of comment by our Lord because its author is, in all miraculous cures, especially concerned to show that our Lord brought the sufferer to believe personally in himself and regarded the miracle as only half done until that was accomplished. The clearest case of that is in John 9:17 and 37, with which compare John 5:8 and 14.

A state of need may be assumed in all who have not come to Christ. The open admission of this need is the next necessity, together with the admission that Christ alone can help. The condition of mind that precludes conversion to him is that in which a man says "I am in no need." But it is equally frustrated by the attitude, "I may be in need, but I'm not going to admit it. I will manage for myself. If he wants to help me, let him come;

but I'm not going to lower myself by asking for him." And even when a need is admitted, and admitted at some personal cost, it will go wrong if the man then says, "Yes, I need what he can give me. But, of course, if he lets me down, if I don't care for what he provides, there's always a second line of defense." It might be anything from classical music to the bottle. Whatever it is, if there is that to fall back on, a man's faith is not undivided, and what Christ has to offer cannot be given.

Now it is a capital mistake to say that faith has nothing to do with the will. It has much to do with it. By the same token, it is a mistake to say that a man must just wait until faith comes, and that there is nothing he can do. Faith is partly a decisive and costly act of the will. Look at the kind of decision any of those eight people had to take in order to set in motion their act of faith. The centurion saying, "I must go myself." The woman with the issue of blood, in that large, chattering, curious crowd saying, "I must tell him." The sinner-woman with her ointment saying, "I must go in and give him this. Goodness knows what they'll say."

Such a decision is always likely to be expensive, and it is always likely to be inhibited by caution, convention, fear of ridicule, fear of public opinion, fear of losing what you already have and being left with nothing. Yes—fear. We come back to "anxiety," insecurity, and all the rest of the ingredients of the sin of the world. This is what holds men back at each stage.

Three things then must be said at once.

First: there is in the passion and resurrection of Christ the boldest possible authentication of the principle that decision is costly, but that it will not let a man down.

"He who descended is he who also ascended far above all the heavens, that he might fill all things" (Eph. 4:10) is not merely an abstract creedal statement. It is the whole pattern of spiritual life. He who was crucified and who rose again has gone, as he said, "to my Father and your Father, to my God and your God" (John 20:17). That is the way we must expect to take—down, and then up.

Second: God does not leave himself without witness (Acts 14:17) in the things of history and everyday life. He does not present men with a mysterious and unintelligible spiritual demand. Common life provides innumerable occasions on which, without reference to any highly religious categories, the technique of faith can be practiced. It is not only toward Christ that costly decisions have to be made. Marriage, business, all human relations are conditions in which a man may live a life whose texture is primarily selfish, or whose texture is primarily self-giving. All human relations have the quality of being able to be poisoned by anxiety and fear and self-regard. Marriages break up on that, business credit evaporates because of that, political systems topple because of nothing else. Wars and disputes come from the desires that are in our members (Jas. 4:1), and those unruly desires are the product of anxious self-regard. At all these points there are for the individual places of repentance, points at which he can bring into action a simple, human, un-self-regarding technique which will so prepare him for the larger decision that its opportunity does not take him unawares. Suppose the traveler had been too morose, too preoccupied with his own concerns to listen to, or even to notice the stranger who had the good news for him? It is at this point, of course, that the social duties of Christians come into the picture. Those social distresses which preoccupy the minds of men, blunt their faculties, and insult their manhood so as to make it impossible for the good news to reach men must be fought and brought down by Christians. No evangelistic message can afford to ignore that.

THE CHURCH

The third thing to be said is also the second main subject of this chapter, namely, that once he sets foot on the road of conversion, the traveler is a member of the church.

When Dr. Graham conducted his evangelistic campaigns in Europe, he always made it clear—all honor to him—that those who were brought to a sense of salvation by his meetings should go at once to a local church. That should always be said. The church we do not see is the whole company of Christian believers, the church we see is constituted in local bodies. It is impossible to fulfil the obligations and enjoy the privileges of conversion without bringing that membership of the church we do not see down to earth by seeking membership in a local church. The converted man is no less in need of his neighbors than the unconverted; he needs a community if he is to fulfil himself.

This is a proposition which many seeking Christians find difficult to accept. "Is it not enough," they say, "that I should believe, and worship God in my own way, and do what good I can to my fellows?" And we accept this objection, and know not what to say.

But it really is a very odd objection. On the face of it, it seems strange that a man who has made a great discovery should avoid the community of people sharing his belief. When he does so, it must be because there is something in the obligations of that society which seems to him heavily to outweigh its privileges.

Well, yes, there is, and that is where the trouble comes. The church, organized in local bodies, has its social and organizational aspects which sometimes appear to make unreasonable demands on its members. "What do I want with all these creeds and covenants?" they say. "I have my faith, that is enough." Very likely you think it is enough. But there are two things to be said that may change your view.

One is very worldly and humanistic. What is real about a religion whose obligations you can fully discharge by associating only with people you like and agree with? You may meet disagreeable people, people of widely different worldly interests in church, and you may have to mix with them and share a cup with them. Are you not taking refuge from that obligation by going off on your own and looking for only the people whom it is easy to live with? Not seldom there is that note in the objection of the people who see no reason why the church should be brought into it.

But, secondly, certain things are promised to the church which are not promised to individuals. Jesus Christ from the beginning founded his ministry on a community—that of the twelve, traitor and all. When Jesus made statements about the coming of the kingdom and the conduct expected of men, he made them in the plural. When he made promises about the continuance of his ministry after his death, he said "If *you* forgive the sins of any, they are forgiven" (John 20:23). And when Paul wrote of the church as the "body of Christ," he meant us to think of it as Christ "embodied" in the world, that is to say, he meant us to learn that the Christ-character and the Christ-work are never promised to any individual, but they are promised to the church.

Society can be redeemed only by a society. The ugly demonic force that makes a crowd in certain circumstances more bestial than any of its individual members must be fought and conquered by the gracious power of the Holy Spirit, which can make Christ's community better and more effective than any of its individual members would be. That the church is often not behaving so is not at all to the point. What matters is that it has been promised that it may be so. The church contains many travelers, some of whom straggle and stumble. But nonetheless, it is the vessel of a power that could not be given to any one person, simply because it is too many-sided and great. The church is not a kindergarten for children, but a school of freedom (II Cor. 3:17). Therefore, naturally, it will have its unattractive and confused outward aspects. But there alone a man can truly find himself, and there alone he can encounter the fortifying rebuke of his neighbor and the friendship of the travelers on their journey. There alone can he come face to face with the broken bread and the poured wine which act out for him again the sacrifice and victory which the Master wrought for him, and which are the normative principle of all life. There alone, in fact, is reality, crude as well as uplifting, homely as well as exalted. Here, perhaps, in words in which Isaac Watts interpreted the Twenty-third Psalm, is the simple truth about all this:

> The sure provisions of my God
>   Attend me all my days;
> O may thy house be mine abode,
>   And all my work be praise;
> There may I find a settled rest
>   While others go and come,
> No more a stranger or a guest,
>   But like a child at home.

"At home" in the church, "at home" in the many-splendored world—that is the promise given to men in Christ.